Food for Thought

The Opus Vegetarian Recipe Book

Leading People give you their Favourite Vegetarian Ideas

By Arnold Baker

Published by
Lord of Barton Publications
The Chippings, Wark, Hexham
Northumberland

'Food for Thought'

Written, Devised, and Published for 'Opus'
by Arnold Baker Esq, Lord of Barton

'First Edition'

'Limited Production of 1000 Copies'

ISBN   0 - 9527708 - 0 - 6

Published by Lord of Barton Publications
The Chippings, Wark, Hexham
Northumberland

Cover Design by
Elliott Design   Tel 0191 5843343

Printed by Bailes the Printer
Mill House, Market Place,
Houghton - Le - Spring,
Tyne & Wear Tel 0191 5846097

Food for Thought

Dedication

This book is dedicated to two doctors who
care for their patients with great compassion
Dr. Graham Maddick, and Dr. Neville Keep
of Wark Surgery, Northumberland.

Also to the staff of 'The Opus Project'.

This is book Number 224
of a Limited Edition of 1000 Copies

The people listed below have helped to produce this book. They share my gratitude

Mick Ackhurst, Barbara Adams, Robert Alnwick, Julie Allen, Pat Allison,   Dave Anderson, Pip Anslow, Rt Hon The Lord Jeffrey Archer,   Jane Asher, Rt. Hon Paddy Ashdown MP, Paula Ball, Carol Banks, Thelma Barlow, Sarah Barnard, Donna Bell, Linda Beavers, Gordon Bentley, Bishops Garages, Rt. Hon Tony Blair MP, Ros Blaylock, Bob Bowey,   Terry Bowey, Richard Branson, Val Brassington, Joy Brayshaw, Dr. Andy Brittlebank,   Prof. Mary Bromley, Robert Brodie, Adrian Brown, Ann Brown, Brian Brown, Cheryl Brown, Hayley Marie Brown, Kevin Brown, Niel Burton, Carol Cairns, Ashlyn Charlton, Tim Chrisp, Catherine Clark, David Clark, John Cleese, Gary Collis, Marie Cook, Ronnie Corbett OBE,   Ellie Craggs Howard Crawford, Gillian Crow, Christine Cullum,   Edwina Currie MP, Jan Daffern,   Hilary Dawson, Paul Davidson, Dennis Davison, Conrad Dickinson, Josceline Dimbleby, Brigita Dobbs, Rachel Dodds, Clare Doody, Christine Down, Chris Edge, Yvonne Edmunds, Ian Elliott, Christine English, Sabastian Coe OBE, MP, Mark Faulder,   Mohamed Al Fayed, Anne Feeley, Sarah Ferguson, Cathy Fisher, Don Fraser, Angela Gilhespy, Stan Graham, Peter Greener, Dr.Hugh Griffith, Peter Hafferty, Leigh Hague, Susan Hamill, Susan Hampshire Hampshire, Dr.Andrea Hearn, Rt. Hon Sir.Edward Heath, Angela Heenan, Lenny Henry, Sue Hepple, David Hepplethwaite, John Herron, Janette Hewison, Suzanne Hills, Mick Hipwell, David Holburn, Sheila Holyoak, Sir. Anthony Hopkins, Dr.Peter Horne, Coun. Bill Howard, Coun. Marion Howard, John Humphrys, Emma Hunter, Faye Hunter, Marilyn Hunter, Gloria Hunniford, Pip Illingworth, David Jacobs, Glenda Jackson MP, Liz Jewitt, Brenda Johnson, Jane Johnson, James Jonas, Gary Kaye, Tina Kaye, Basil Kohlak, Sue Law, Neel Lever Mike Neville MBE, Ann Liddon, Malcolm Lloyd, Caroline Luke, Pat Lumsden, Sylvia Maddison, David Madge, Sam Makin, Linda McCartney, Jon McDonnell,   Steve McKuskin, Jackie McNulty, Ian Maltby, Rt. Hon. John Major MP, Christopher Melges, Dr. Middleton, Steph Middleton, Beborah Mileham, Garry Millard, Spike Milligan,   Jonathan Mood, Doreen Mollison, Gillian Mordain, Wico Van Mooric, Ellen Nixon, Ruth O'Meara, Tony Parker Tony Pape, Sue Townsend, Mike Parry, Dawn Parkinson, Billy Paxton, Wendy Phillips, Lee Phillipson, Mieke Pickard, Jennifer Pickering, Avril Pickering, Luke Pickering, Jon Pickering, Lester Piggiott, Margaret Porter, Lady Baden - Powell, Margaret Punshon, John Purvis, Mick Quinn, Leslie Ramsey, Claire Rayner, David Reay, Angela Reed, John Reed, Cheryl Reily Sir.Ciff Richard, Eileen Richardson, Dr. Esti Rimmer, Ian Robinson,   Robert Robinson Alan Robson MBE, Bill Robson, Deirdre Robson, Judith Rochester,   Marilyn Ross, Janice Routledge, Pam Royle, Bob Sackley, Caroline Sackley, Michael Sanderson, Graham Scott Jackie Sewell, Peter Sissons, Helen Smart, Steve Shrubb, Jill Slorance,   Bill Smith, Margaret Smith, Brenda Spence, Meg Stokoe, Joanna Strachan, Christine Swalwell,   Ernie Swinburn Jo Swinburn, Sylvia Swinburn, Lindsay Taylor, Bill Tarmey, Rt.Hon.Lady Margaret Thatcher Elenor Thew, Debbie Thrower, Gill Town, Jon Trueman, Caroline Tully, Anthea Turner, Jean Turner, Lord David Ainger-Turner, Anne Unger, Lady Melody Urquart, Kate Vince, Terry Waite CBE, David Walton, George Wharrier, Paul White, Sara White, Stuart White, June Whitfield, Julia Whitehead, Eric Wilkie, Susan Wilkinson, Gail Williams, John Williamson Colin Wilson, Craig Wilson, Julie Wintrip, HRH The Duchess of York,   Lorna Younger

Introduction

The ancient and historic market town called Hexham lies not a stones throw from the majestic river Tyne, and the once mighty Roman Wall. The great historic significance of it's ancient Abbey, Moot Hall, and Market Place, has drawn visitors to the town for well over a thousand years. Many of these visitors have no doubt enjoyed the friendship of the Hexham folk, and the hospitality of the towns hostelrys.

Hexham is still a magnet to visitors from neighbouring towns and villages and for tourists from all parts of the globe. It is hoped that these visitors leave the town with pleasant memories. In recent years, there has been several significant improvements to the heart of the town. The opening up of the old St. Marys Chare has greatly improved the town. St. Marys Chare is now important for several reasons, not least because it is the home for the 'Opus Project' and the Hexham Tans Restaurant.

The Opus Project is special, it is unique!. Having been set up by the Northumberland Mental Health Trust in June 1993, to see if something could be done to help people who have experienced mental health problems to return to worthwhile employment. Right from the start the project began to see some success due to the caring approach, and commitment of every-one who was involved.

The Opus Project is now well established, and set to go on from strength to strength, doing a most worthwhile job for the people of Hexham and surrounding areas. An integral part, if you like, showcase of the project is the Hexham Tans Vegetarian Restaurant, also in St. Marys Chare, where visitors enjoy fine vegetarian food in a very comfortable setting. Everyone is made equally welcome by the friendly and efficient staff.

The Opus Project, and Hexham Tans restaurant have been a success due to the hard work and commitment of the 'Opus Team', Ernie Swinburn, Jon Pickering, Hayley Brown, and Sara White, and the support and encouragement of Northumberland Mental Health Trust. This book is a tribute to them.

In buying this book, you may be pleased to know that every penny that you have given has gone directly to Opus to help to ensure their continuance. The book has been paid for by sponsors who's help is very gratefully appreciated and acknowledged. The many famous and important people who are featured in this book may not themselves be vegetarians. What is important is the fact that these people have demonstrated in a most practical way that they care. The fact that so many such people have come forward to embrace the project is very gratefully acknowledged.

I hope that you enjoy the book, and have a go at making some of the recipes. Please tell all of your friends about the Opus Project, and the wonderful work that they are doing. Better still buy them a copy of this book. Please befriend and support the 'Opus Project' if you can.

10 DOWNING STREET
LONDON SW1A 2AA

THE PRIME MINISTER

I am pleased to acknowledge the valuable contribution made by OPUS to the rehabilitation of those recovering from mental health problems. This work supports our aim to improve community care for people with a mental illness to which the Government attaches a high priority.

John Major

The Opus Project by Ernie Swinburn

One in four of us will need to seek professional help for a mental health problem at some time during our lives. It can happen to anyone, young or old, and it could happen to you. This kind of problem may be organic, or can be triggered by events in a person's life, such as bereavement or unexpected redundancy.

When problems like this do happen, there are well qualified professionals who will provide clinical help, but returning to work can be more difficult. That is why Northumberland Mental Health NHS Trust has a range of work experience schemes, to help people get over this hurdle. The Opus Project in Tynedale is one part of that and, uniquely, operates the Hexham Tans as a real business in the high street. Our mission statement is. "Assisting people with mental health problems to attain their maximum in worthwhile work", and that is what we try to do.

Of course, as you will realise, anything worthwhile is usually difficult to achieve, and we have had our share of difficulties, but this is more than offset by successes as we see people move on through the project, to a whole spectrum of different kinds of work. I have on my wall a framed, handwritten message from one of these people. It reads: "Nothing great was ever achieved without enthusiasm". Whenever I need reminding, I look at it.

Thank you for buying this book, and for helping us to continue in our work. Please come to the Tans Restaurant and enjoy the food. If you ask a member of staff we will be pleased to show you around the project, and tell you more about it. Enjoy the book.

Some messages of support

"Every success for this wonderful project and continued good luck for the future". Rt. Hon The Lord Archer.,   "I wish you every success with your fund raising". Rt. Hon. Paddy Ashdown MP.   " With very best wishes for every success to the Opus Project" Jane Asher.,   "Good Luck" Thelma Barlow.,   " Kind regards, and best wishes to Opus".   Rt. Hon. Tony Blair MP.,   "Best of luck with your project". Richard Branson.,   "Good luck with your project" Dame Katherine Cookson DBE, and Mr. Tom Cookson.,   " Best wishes to the Opus Project" Ronnie Corbett OBE, "Good luck with the book and the fund raising"   Josceline Dimbleby   "I wish the Opus Project every success in it's future worthwhile work for the Hexham community".   Susan Hampshire.,   "Every good wish". Rt. Hon. Sir Edward Heath KG MBE, MP.,   "This is an admirable project, I certainly wish you every success". David Holburn.,   "May I offer you every good wish with Opus. It deserves to succeed".   John Humphrys.,   "I send my best wishes to Opus".   Gloria Hunniford.,   "Good luck, and my very best wishes to all concerned with the Opus Project".   Glenda Jackson MP.,   "With all good wishes for the success of your project".   Rt. Hon. John Major MP., Prime Minister,.   " I wish Opus ever y success with raising funds".   Linda McCartney.,   "Good luck with this project".   Spike Milligan.,   "Good luck with your recipe book - may it's success bring more success to Opus".   Mike Neville MBE.,   " This seems a very worthy cause and I wish you every success".   His Grace The Duke of Northumberland.,   "Kind regards". Lester Piggott.,   "I send all connected with the Opus Project every good wish".   The Lady Patience Baden - Powell CBE.,   "We should all help whenever we can. These people make a difference and have my full support".   Alan Robson MBE.,   " Here's hoping that the book is a great success and raises a huge amount for Opus".   Claire Rayner.,   "I am sure the publication will be a great accomplishment for the Opus Project".   David Reay.,   "Wishing Opus every success in the work that it is doing now and in the future".   Pam Royle.,   "I wish you luck with your project".   Peter Sissons.,   "I wish every success with the book, and the Opus Project".   Bill Tarmey "I congratulate you on all you are doing, and wish you all the best for the project" Rt. Hon. Lady Margaret Thatcher OM, PC, FRS.,   "With best wishes to the project, hoping you'll go from strength to strength".   Debbie Thrower,.   "Best wishes to everyone connected with Opus. I hope that the book will be a great success".   Sue Townsend.,   "I hope that the book is a great success".   Anthea Turner.,   "With all good wishes".   Terry Waite CBE.,   "Best wishes to Opus".   June Whitfield OBE.,   "Her Royal Highness has asked me to convey her best wishes".   Hilary Bett, Personal Secretary to HRH The Duchess of York.

The Opus Team

Hayley Marie Brown, Trainer - Support Co-ordinator, and Ernie Swinburn Project Manager

Sara White, the Opus Chef, and Jon Pickering, Project Manager.

Index

Sponsorship of this book

**The entire production cost of this book has been met through sponsorship. This means
that ever penny raised through the sale of this book goes directly to the Opus Trust.
The Opus Trust very gratefully acknowledges the sponsors generosity.
A list of sponsors is shown on the back cover of this book.**

Quick Guide

Every recipe in this book has with it a series of 'Quick Guide' letters. This enables the reader to see at a glance some important features of that recipe. These 'Quick Guide' letters are listed below. <u>In the interests of safety please ensure that children are closely supervised in the kitchen.</u>

A   Advanced Preparation

B   Bake in the Oven

C   Easy for Children

D   Difficult

E   Easy

F   Freezes well

G   Grill required

N   Naughty but nice

O   Optional extras

T   Technical

Q   Quick

X   Contains Alcohol

Watercress Soup

Kathy Secker

Ingredients

3 oz (75g) of Butter

_____

1 Small Onion

_____

2 Bunches of Watercress

_____

1 Large Potato

_____

1 3/4 pints (150ml) of Vegetable Stock

_____

1/4 pt (150ml) of Single Cream

_____

Black Pepper to taste

_____

Salt to taste

_____

Description

A good quality, all year round soup that is so quick, and easily made. Serve it with crispy bread or croutons & enjoy.

Method

Stage 1

Chop the Onion into medium sized pieces. Slice the Potato, then cut into small cubes. Wash, trim, and roughly chop the watercress Make up the 1 3/4 pts of Vegetable Stock using Stock Cubes if necessary.

Stage 2

Melt 1 oz of Butter in a pan, add the Onion and gently simmer until it is translucent, (do not let it brown). Add the remaining Butter saute for approximately 5 minutes.

Stage 3

Add the potato, and cook for another couple of minutes, then remove from the heat. Stir in the Vegetable Stock. Season to taste with Salt and Black Pepper.

Stage 4

Return to the heat, bring to the boil, then simmer for 25 / 30 minutes. Cool slightly then liquidise. Transfer to a clean pan to re-heat. Serve with a swirl of Fresh Single Cream.

Quick Guide

C E F O Q

Lentil Soup with Lemon

Glenda Jackson MP

Ingredients

8 oz of Split Red Lentils

_____

2 Pints of Vegetable Stock

_____

1 Large Onion

_____

1 Small (8 oz) tin of Tomatoes

_____

2 Cloves of Crushed Garlic

_____

1 oz of Butter or Margarine

_____

Small quantity of Lemon Juice

_____

1 Teaspoon of Cumin & Salt and
Pepper to taste

Description

Lentil soup is always a firm favourite for most families.
This soup is differenced by adding a twist of Lemon.

Method

Stage 1

Soak 8 oz of Red Split Lentils in cold water overnight
to allow them to swell.

Stage 2

Drain the softened Lentils, and wash them in cold water.
Put into a large pan with the 2 pints of Vegetable Stock.

Stage 3

Finely chop the Onion, and gently fry it in the 1 oz of
Butter or Margarine in a frying pan until it is softened then
add it to the pan with the tinned Tomato and Crushed
Garlic. Stir well.

Stage 4

Put pan on heat and bring the soup to the boil then simmer
for 30 - 45 minutes or until the lentils are softened. Allow
to cool slightly, then liquidise in a blender (or not if more
chunky soup is preferred)

Stage 5

Return to the pan then add the Cumin, and Seasoning.
Stir well and add the Lemon juice. Serve with a thin slice
of Lemon floating on the top to garnish.

Quick Guide

A   C   E   F

Leek and Potato Soup

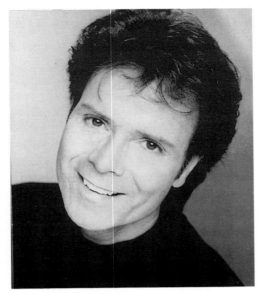

Sir. Cliff Richard O.B.E.

<u>Ingredients</u>

2 x Large Onions

1 x lb of Potatoes

1/2 lb of Fresh Leaks

Mixed Herbs (to taste)

2 oz of Butter

1/4 pint of Natural Yoghurt

2 Pints of Vegetable Stock
(3 x Vegetable Stock Cubes)

A quick and tasty soup which keeps this 'Bachelor Boy'
fit and begging for more !

Method

Stage 1

Peel Potatoes, and cut into small chunks. Chop
Onions roughly, cut Leeks into small segments.

Stage 2

Melt the Butter in a large pan and saute
the Potatoes and Onions for a few minutes

Stage 3

Add the Vegetable Stock, Herbs and Leeks
(Stock made up from 3 x Vegetable Stock
Cubes and Two Pints of Boiling Water will do)

Stage 4

Bring to boil, and simmer until the Potatoes are
cooked and soft. Allow to cool for ten minutes

Stage 5

Stir Yoghurt into the soup. With very great care
put the soup through a blender at maximum speed
until it is pureed. Add Salt to taste if required

Serve Hot or Cold as desired. Serves 4 - 5

Quick Guide

C   E   F   Q

Chilled Fennel and Pepper Soup

Jane Asher

<u>Ingredients</u>

3 Tablespoons of Sunflower Oil

---

1 Large Onion

---

1 Large Orange Pepper

---

1 Large Yellow Pepper

---

570 ml (1 pt) Good Quality Vegetable Stock

Salt and Freshly Ground Pepper

1.1 kg / 2 1/2 lb Florence Fennel
(reserve the green fronds)

Description

This is a really 'First Class' Chilled Soup. An ideal
starter for almost any mid summer dinner party

Method

Stage 1

Deseed Peppers and chop into small pieces reserving
a slice of each. Chop Fennel (reserving green fronds)
Chop Onion into small pieces.

Stage 2

Heat the Oil in a large heavy based pan. Add Fennel
and Onions, and cook over a gentle heat for 5
minutes or until softened but not coloured.

Stage 3

Add the chopped Peppers to the pan, turn the heat
up to medium, and cook for 10 minutes, stirring
occasionally.

Stage 4

Add the 1 pt of Good Quality Vegetable Stock.
and 1 pt of Cold Water, then season to taste with
Salt and freshly ground White Pepper. Bring to the
boil, reduce the heat and simmer for 20 minutes
until the Peppers have softened.

Stage 5

Allow to cool, then pour the mixture into a blender or
food processor and puree until smooth. Cover & chill

Garnish

Cut the reserved strips of Pepper into fine slivers and
use a little of each colour to garnish the soup along
with the reserved fronds of Fennel.

Quick Guide

Carrot and Sweet Potato Soup

Rt Hon Tony Blair MP

Ingredients

1 Medium Onion - 3 Large Carrots

1 Large Sweet Potato - 1/2 Pint of Milk

1 Tablespoon of Chopped fresh Coriander

1/2 a Pint of Fresh Orange Juice

1/2 a Pint of Vegetable Stock

1 Tablespoon of Olive Oil

Freshly ground Black Pepper

Salt to taste

A very interesting but quickly made soup.   Just the thing
for someone who is going places, and is too busy to
spend a great deal of time in the kitchen.

Method

Stage 1

Finely chop up all of the Vegetables

Stage 2

Put the Olive Oil in a Large Pan and
heat. Add the Chopped Vegetables
and cook in the Oil until softened but
not browned.

Stage 3

Add the Vegetable Stock and Orange
Juice.   Stir well,   cover and allow to
simmer gently for 1 hour.

Stage 4

Put into a blender and puree until smooth
Return to Pan. Add Milk and reheat.

Stage 5

Season to taste with Black Pepper
and Salt. If Soup is too think dilute
slightly using additional Stock. Serve

Garnish

Garnish with finely chopped Coriander

C   E   F   Q

Mushroom Soup

June Whitfield OBE

Ingredients

4 Tablespoons of Butter

_____

1 Tablespoon of Flour

_____

1 Pint of Vegetable Stock

_____

1/2 Pint of Milk

_____

3/4 lb of Mushrooms

_____

2 Tablespoons of Fresh Parsley

_____

The juice of half a Lemon

_____

1/4 Pint of Double Cream

_____

Salt and Pepper to season

Description

This Mushroom Soup is very quickly made. It is slightly different from many other mushroom soups because of the added Lemon Juice which perks it up.

Method

Stage 1

Wash your Mushrooms well in cold water then slice them up fairly finely. Wash the Parsley, and chop it up. Make up your 1 pint of Vegetable Stock using vegetable stock cubes as directed on the packet.

Stage 2

Put the 4 Tablespoons of Butter into a medium sized pan. Warm the pan gently on the stove to melt the Butter, the add the Flour, stir, and allow this mixture to cook very gently for 2 minutes.

Stage 3

Add the sliced Mushrooms, and Parsley. Bring up the heat, then add the Stock, Milk, and Lemon Juice stirring together well. Bring almost to the boiling point, but do not boil, then simmer for 5 minutes.

Stage 4

Remove pan from the heat, allow the soup to cool slightly, then carefully place into a liquidiser to puree. If you do not possess a liquidiser put the soup through a fine meshed sieve.

Stage 5

Return to the pan to reheat. When the soup is nearing the boil, but not boiling, add the Fresh Cream. Stir and season to taste. Serve whilst still hot.

Quick Guide

C · E · F · N · Q

Tangy Rice Salad

David Jacobs

Ingredients

4 Cups of Fluffy Rice

_____

1 Tablespoon of Vinegar

_____

1 Teaspoon of Lemon Juice

_____

1 Tablespoon of Light Oil

_____

1/4 Teaspoon of Tumeric

_____

1/2 Teaspoon of Cayenne Pepper

_____

3/4 Cup of Raisins

_____

1/3 Cup of Chopped Green Peppers

Continued.....

2 Tablespoons of Chutney

2/3 Cup of Yoghurt or Sour Cream

2/3 Cup of Mayonnaise

Chopped Fresh Coriander

---

6 Slices of Lime

---

2 Teaspoons of Curry Powder
Hot, Medium or Mild according to taste

Description

The great number of ingredients in this salad gives it a really nice tangy taste. It's ideal as a starter or as part of a main meal. The above quantities are for 6 persons

Method

Stage 1

Chop the Green Pepper, and Chutney up into very small pieces. Chop the Fresh Coriander and slice the Lime into thin slices.

Stage 2

Boil the Rice until it is soft and fluffy. Whist the Rice is still hot, transfer it to a mixing bowl and sprinkle it with the Vinegar, Oil, and Lemon Juice. Mix lightly, add the Tumeric and the Cayenne then blend in gently. Stir in the Raisins, Green Peppers and Chutney. Add the Yoghurt (or Sour Cream) and Mayonnaise. Mix together very well so that everything is evenly spread.

Stage 3

Share out evenly into 6 Buttered Ramekins. Press down lightly in the mould, refrigerate for at least one hour. To serve unmould onto a bed of fresh lettuce. Decorate with the chopped Coriander and a slice of Lime.

Quick Guide

A   C   E   O   Q

Avocado Salad

Pam Royle

Ingredients

2 Large Avocados

The Juice of a Lemon

---

2 Tomatoes

---

2 Sticks of Celery

1/2 Red Pepper (skinned)

1/2 An Onion or 1 Shallot

---

1 Dessert spoon of finely chopped Parsley

---

2 Table Spoons of Double Cream

Freshly Ground Black Pepper, and Sea Salt to taste.

Description

This is a great starter, or if you serve it with thin slices
of mature Cheddar Cheese it's a light main meal.

Method

Stage 1
Halve the Avocados lengthways. Remove the stones and scoop
out the inner flesh leaving a little on the skin to leave a firm shell.

Stage 2
Rub a little of the Lemon Juice on the inner surface of
the shells to prevent discoloration.

Stage 3
Cut the removed centres of the Avocados into small cubes,
place in a bowl and stir in the rest of the Lemon Juice

Stage 4
Skin & deseed Tomatoes, then chop them into small pieces

Stage 5
Chop the Celery, Red Pepper and Onion into small pieces,
and add these ingredients, and the chopped Tomatoes to
the Avocado in the bowl.

Stage 6
Finely chop Parsley. Add the Parsley, Double Cream and
Seasoning to the bowl. (also Garlic if desired)

Stage 7
Combine the mixture well, (mix well). It will thicken and
make it's own salad dressing.

Stage 8
Fill the Avocado shells, and chill before serving.

Quick Guide

A C E N O

Susan's Salad

Susan Hampshire

<u>Ingredients</u>

Lettuce or Chicory

_____

1 Chopped Banana

_____

2 Grated Carrots

_____

2 Sliced Tomatoes

_____

A handful of Raisins - 6 Almonds

_____

1/4 lb Strawberries or Pineapple

_____

Grated Ginger Root (optional)

_____

6 oz of Cottage Cheese
or Mild Goats Cheese

Description

A fruity, fresh tasting salad, which will
set your taste buds wild with desire.

Salad Dressing

Small quantity of fresh Chopped Chives

Small quantity of fresh Parsley

---

3 Tablespoons of Walnut Oil

Onion Salt and Ground Pepper to taste

---

1 Teaspoon of Cider Vinegar
or Lemon Juice

Method

Stage 1
Arrange a bed of Lettuce or Chicory onto two plates.

Stage 2
Arrange all of the remaining ingredients on top of the
bed of Lettuce or Chicory

Stage 3
Grate Ginger Root onto Cottage or Goats Cheese

Stage 4
Put ingredients of Dressing into a tightly sealed bottle
shake vigorously, sprinkle onto salad, serve at once

Quick Guide

C   E   O   Q

John Humphrys Salad Dressing

John Humphrys

Ingredients

8 Tablespoons of good quality Olive Oil

2 Tablespoons of Balsamic Vinegar

2 Tablespoons of Cider Vinegar

2 Teaspoons of English Mustard

'far too much' Garlic

Salt to taste

Description

A salad dressing which is quickly made. John say's,
"Since I'm not a cook it's all very hit-and-miss"

Method

Stage 1

Crush the juice from far-too-much Garlic into
a measuring jug. Add the Olive Oil, Balsamic
Vinegar, Cider Vinegar, English Mustard,
and Salt (to taste)

Stage 2

Transfer ingredients into a tightly sealed bottle
shake vigorously until well mixed. Slosh over
just about everything !

Quick Guide

A C E O Q

****

John Cleese Breakfast Dish

Submitted by John Cleese

Ingredients

Cornflakes

Fresh Milk or Coca-Cola

Description

It's very simple to make and absolutely delicious. An alternative
is to use Coca-Cola instead of Milk. Also add 'Basil' if required

Method

Buy a packet of Cornflakes, and some milk. Open the cardboard
box. Open the sort of plastic packet inside the box. Put the contents
(sort of yellowy brownish bits of things) into a bowl. Take the top
off the thin end of the bottle. Invert bottle gently over the Cornflakes
Making sure that the milk does not go over the edge of the plate.

Quick Guide

C E N Q

The 'Tans' Vegetarian Restaurant

The home of fine vegetarian food in the heart of Hexham Town Centre

Very comfortable surroundings, and a warm welcome awaits all visitors to the 'Tans' Vegetarian Restaurant, in St Marys Chare

Cheddar Cheese Souffle

Submitted by Lester Piggott

Ingredients

1 1/2 oz of Plain Flour

_____

1 1/2 oz of Butter

_____

3 Egg Yolks

_____

Egg Whites

_____

1/2 Pint of Milk

_____

3 oz of Strong Cheddar Cheese

_____

Salt, Pepper, Mustard to taste

Description

Cheese Souffle is very popular as a starter, or part of a main meal.

Method

Stage 1

Pre-heat the oven to 350 f, 180c, Gas Mark 4/5. Separate the Egg Yolks from the Egg Whites. Grate the Cheese.

Stage 2

Whisk the Egg Whites until they are very stiff and form peaks. Beat the Egg Yolks. Melt the Butter in a saucepan, gradually stir in the flour. Add the Milk gradually, whilst stirring, allow the mixture to thicken, then add the seasoning to taste, and the grated Cheese

Stage 3

Remove from the heat, and add the beaten Egg Yolks, stir, then add the well beaten egg Whites, fold into the mixture. Pour it into a Souffle Dish, then immediately bake in the oven for 35 minutes

Quick Guide

B   T   Q

Pasta with Two Cheeses

Rt Hon Paddy Ashdown MP

Ingredients

1 Large Tin of Plum Tomatoes (15oz / 375g)

---

1 Clove of Garlic, (Finely Chopped.)

---

1 Tablespoon of Olive Oil (any oil will do)

---

2 Teaspoons of Dried Basil or 5 fresh Basil Leaves

---

2 oz / 50g   Mature Cheddar Cheese.

---

5 oz / 125g   Mozzarella Cheese,

Any sort of Pasta. Read the instructions on packet
to determine quantity required for two people

Description

A pasta meal in which you can use your own flair and imagination by mixing two or three pasta's if you choose. This is one of Paddy's family's favourite supper dishes, but it could be a main course, or snack.

Method

Stage 1

Put a large pan of water on to boil, add a small quantity of salt, When the water boils, add the pasta and cook it until it is cooked (Usually about 10 minutes, see instructions on packet)

Stage 2

In a heavy based pan, mash the tomatoes with the back of a wooden spoon, add the Olive Oil, Basil, and Garlic, and simmer gently so that the sauce heats, and thickens.

Stage 3

Whilst Pasta and Sauce are cooking, grate the Cheddar Cheese, Cut the Mozzarella Cheese into small cubes. Add both cheeses to the sauce, stir once, then turn the heat well down. Simmer very slowly for 1 minute. If the sauce sticks, remove from the heat, and cover with lid to keep hot until pasta is cooked.

Stage 4

Once the Pasta is cooked, drain well, put onto two plates, then add the sauce, serve immediately with crisp 'Green Salad'

Serves 2 persons

C E F O Q

Summer Stew with Vegetables

Linda McCartney

Ingredients

2 Heaped tbs of Cornflower, mixed with 3 tbs of Water

1 x 14 oz (400g) can of Chopped Tomatoes with Juice

3 - 4 tbs of Fresh Parsley, Thyme, Tarragon or other Mixed Herbs

Optional Spices to taste -- 3 tbs of Vegetable Oil

1 Large Onion -- 1 Large Clove of Garlic

8 oz of Vegetarian Steak Chunks -- 2 tbs of Olive Oil

6 oz (175g) of Young Carrots -- 1 Baby Turnip

6 oz (175g) of Cauliflower Florets

1 Pint of Vegetable Stock

Continued.......

6 oz (175g) of New Potatoes

---

8 oz (250g) of Baby Courgettes

Sea Salt and freshly ground Pepper to taste

Description

A satisfying stew for people who don't want to eat meat but still like it's texture. You can of course vary the vegetables and alter the seasoning to suit your own taste.

Method

Stage 1

Make up your Vegetable Stock. Finely chop the Parsley, Thyme, Tarragon or other Mixed Herbs. Peel and finely chop the Onion, Garlic, and New Potatoes. Slice the baby Corgettes, and Carrots. Cube the Turnip, and the Vegetar -ian Steak. Break the Cauliflower into small florets.

Stage 2

In a large pan, covered on a low heat, soften the Onion and Garlic in the Olive Oil. Then add the prepared Vegetables and brown for 5 - 6 minutes stirring and turning continuously Gradually add the Stock, stirring, bring to the boil, then stir in the Cornflower and Water mixture. Add the Tomatoes with their juice and stir well. Add the herbs, plus any spices that you choose. Season to taste.

Stage 3

Turn the heat right down, and cover the pan tightly. Simmer gently for 25 minutes, stirring occasionally. Meanwhile heat the Vegetable Oil in a shallow pan and brown the Vegetarian Steak Cubes all over for about 3 minutes. Then stir the steak cubes into the stew. Cover again and cook gently for a further 10 mins. Check the Seasoning. It's now ready to eat.

Quick Guide

C E F O Q

Roasted Red Peppers with Grilled Goats Cheese

The Rt. Hon. John Major MP
Prime Minister

<u>Ingredients</u>

4 Red Peppers

_____

A small quantity of Fresh Spinach Leaves

_____

Balsamic Vinegar

_____

Black Pepper to taste if required

_____

Salt to taste if required

_____

2 Tubular Goats Cheeses
not too short (approx. 4 oz each)

_____

Description

A dish with a rare European flavour. It's beauty is in it's simplicity. It is quickly made, so it serves as a light snack, starter, or as part of a main meal.

Method

Stage 1

Cut the Red Peppers lengthways into quarters with a sharp knife. Remove the seeds and the pith then wash them thoroughly. Cut the tubular goats cheeses into about four discs from each cheese.

Stage 2

Light the Grill and turn it up to it's highest setting. Whilst it is heating wash and dry the Spinach and arrange it decoratively onto four plates.

Stage 3

Place the quartered Peppers skin side up on a baking tray (with a lip to collect the juices) Sear the Peppers under the grill until they are blackened. Remove from the grill and wrap in a clean tea towel, and allow them to cool until they can be handled. The burnt skins should then slip off. Reserve the juices from the baking tray.

Stage 4

Place the cut discs of Goats Cheese into the grill on the baking tray until they are bubbling and brown. Then remove from the grill.

Stage 5

Place four quarters of warm Pepper on top of the Spinach on each plate. Add two discs of the grilled Goats Cheese. Dribble each serving with Balsamic Vinegar and any reserved juices. Grind a little Black Pepper and Salt onto the meal if required. Serve this meal whilst still hot.

Quick Guide

C   E   G   Q

Vegetable Pie, A recipe from Ireland

Gloria Hunniford

<u>Ingredients</u>

40g / 1 1/2 oz of Butter,

___

40 g / 1 1/2 oz of Plain Flour

___

225g / 8oz of Carrots -- 1 beaten Egg, to glaze

___

100 g / 4 oz of Frozen Broad Beans

___

1 Onion Sliced -- Salt and Pepper to taste

___

300 ml / 10 fl oz of Vegetable Stock

___

175 g / of Shortcrust Pastry -- 1 Small Cauliflower

___

30 ml / 2 tbsp. of Fresh Parsley

___

225 g / 8 oz of Swede or Turnip

Description

Gloria has kindly submitted this recipe from Ireland. It brings back memories of her childhood on the farm in County Armagh when she was always sure of good wholesome home made food

Method

Stage 1

Pre-heat the oven to Gas Mark 6, 200c / 400f. Make up the Vegetable Stock. Make up the Short Crust Pastry.

Stage 2

Peel and thinly slice the Carrots, Peel the Swede or Turnip then cut it up into small dice. Slice the Onion finely. Break up the Cauliflower into small florets. Finely chop up the Parsley.

Stage 3

Put a large frying pan onto heat, add the Butter, when it is melted add the Carrots, Swede or Turnip, & Onion. Cook for 8 minutes. Then add the Flour, stir well, and cook for a further minute. Then gradually add the Stock bring back to the boil stirring continuously. Add the Cauliflower, Beans, Parsley, and the Salt and Pepper to taste. Mix together well. Transfer to a 900 ml / 1.2 litre / 1 1/2 Pint Oven-proof Pie Dish.

Stage 4

On a lightly floured surface, roll out the Shortcrust Pastry until it is 2" / 5cm wider than the pie dish. Cut a strip about 1" / 2.5 cm wide off the side of the rolled out Pastry. Wet the edge of the pie dish with water, then run the 1" pastry strip around the edge of the pie dish. Wet this strip slightly, then using a rolling pin, apply the pastry topping to the pie. Crimp the edges firmly to seal. Cut off any overhanging pastry. Use any of the left over pastry for applied decoration to the pie crust if desired. Cut a hole in the crust top to allow any steam to escape. Brush the top with beaten egg to glaze. Then bake in the oven for 45 minutes or until the crust is golden.

Quick Guide

B   C   E   F   O   Q

Beef in Two Mustard and Tarragon Sauce

Bill Tarmey

Ingredients

2 1/4 lbs of Vegetarian Beef

1 Large Sliced Onion

4 oz of Butter or Margarine

2 Tablespoons of Cooking Oil

1 Tablespoon of Plain Flour

1/2 Pint of Guinness

1 Tablespoon of English Mustard

1 Tablespoon of Mild French Mustard

List of Ingredients continued

1 Tablespoon of Chopped Fresh Tarragon

---

1 Teaspoon of Caster Sugar

Salt and Black Pepper to taste

1/4 Pint of Double Cream

---

3 Large Slices of White Bread

A few sprigs of Fresh Tarragon to Garnish

Description

This is one of Bill's favourite meals. It takes 20 minutes to prepare, 40 minutes to cook, and only a very short time to eat when shared out between 6 persons. It's Magic !

Method

Stage 1

Finely chop the Fresh Tarragon. Thinly slice the Onion, cut the Vegetarian Steak into smallish cubes.

Stage 2

Melt half of the Butter in a Large Shallow Pan, add the Onion and fry it in the Butter for 3 - 4 minutes. Then add the cubed Vegetarian Steak, continue to fry until the Steak is coloured on all sides. Stir in the Flour and gradually add the Guinness. Bring to the boil stirring continuously and add the two Mustards, Tarragon, Sugar, and Salt and Pepper.

Stage 3

Cover and simmer gently for 30 minutes until the Vegetarian Steak is tender. Meanwhile, remove the crusts from bread and cut each slice into eight triangles. Fry in the remaining Butter until crisp and golden. Drain and keep in a warm place. Stir the Cream into the Vegetarian Steak. Allow it to heat through. Spoon onto a serving dish, arrange the bread croutons around the edge. Garnish with Tarragon.

Quick Guide.

C   E   F   N   X

The Opus Potato and Asparagus Gratin

Sara White, Opus Chef

Ingredients

2 lb of Potatoes

1 lb of Asparagus

2 - 3 Cloves of Garlic

1 Pint of Double Cream

1 oz of Butter

Freshly Ground Black Pepper

Salt

Description

As you would expect, Sara has given you this top quality recipe. It's fairly easy to make, and full of the very best ingredients. Serve it with a tossed green Salad and Crispy Bread, Wonderful ! (serves 4)

Method

Stage 1

Preheat the oven to Gas Mark 2, 300 f, 150 c.

Stage 2

Peel and slice the potatoes as thinly as possible. Cut the Asparagus into short lengths. Chop up the Butter into small pieces. Crush the 2 - 3 Cloves of Garlic.

Stage 3

Butter the inside of a Gratin Dish. Then start by placing some of the thinly sliced Potato onto the base of the Gratin dish ensuring that the whole base is covered. Sprinkle with Salt, and Pepper, and some of the Crushed Garlic. Place Some of the Asparagus pieces on top of the Potato layer then season again.

Stage 4

Keep on layering the Potato and Asparagus in this fashion, not forgetting to season each layer as you go until all of the Potato, and Asparagus is in the dish. Pour in the Double Cream, then dot the top with the Butter pieces.

Stage 5

Cover the top of the Gratin dish with baking foil, and bake the dish in the oven for 1 1/2 hours. Remove the foil, then turn the oven temperature up to Gas Mark 4 350 f, 180 c, for about 10 minutes to brown the top.

Quick Guide

B C E F N

Traditional Cornish Pasty

Sebastian Coe OBE, MP.

Ingredients

10 oz of Shortcrust Pastry

_____

1 Medium sized Onion

_____

8 oz of Turnip or Swede

_____

Salt and Pepper to taste

_____

A knob of Butter

_____

4 oz of Potatoes

_____

4 oz of Carrots

_____

8 oz of Vegetarian Mince
(optional extra)

Description

An ideal meal for someone who is always running. The Cornish Pasty can be a main course, or snack. In Cornwall "come aboard" pasty replaces the meat with extra vegetables. If these pasty's are to be made without the Vegetarian Mince, the amounts of vegetables are correct.If you want to incorporate the Vegetarian Mince into the recipe you must reduce the vegetables by a total of 8 oz. Leeks can be used instead of Onions if preferred.

Method

Stage 1

Wash all of the Vegetables in cold water. Peel and cut the Vegetables into very small pieces. Put into a mixing bowl, add the vegetarian mince if desired. Season to taste, then stir together well to evenly distribute the ingredients.

Tip. A little Vegetable Stock may be added to increase the moisture content but great care should be taken in doing this or the juices will run.

Stage 2

Roll out your Shortcrust Pastry onto a cutting board to a thickness of just over 1/8 of an inch. Using a sharp knife, cut out four circles of pastry about 6 " or 15cm in diameter.

Stage 3

Place the mixed filling in the centre of the pastry and then fold it over to form half moon shapes. Moisten the edges, and then crimp them together firmly. Put a small slit in the top to allow the steam to escape. Brush the top with beaten Egg or Milk to glaze.

Stage 4

Bake on a lightly greased baking sheet, in a hot oven 200c or 400f for 30 minutes until pale brown then turn the heat down to 180c 350f, and continue to bake for a further 25 to 30 minutes. If the top is turning brown too quickly cover with aluminium foil to prevent burning

Quick Guide

B C E F O Q

Leek and Macaroni Au Gratin

Terry Waite CBE

Ingredients

175g (6 oz) of short cut Macaroni

_____

75g (3 oz) Butter or Margarine

_____

350g (12oz) of fresh Leeks

_____

40g (1. 1/2oz) Flour

_____

900ml (1. 1/2 pints) of Milk

_____

225g (8oz) of Double Gloucester Cheese

_____

Salt and Pepper to taste

_____

40g (1/1/2oz) of fresh Breadcrumbs

_____

30ml (2 Tbsp) of snipped fresh Chives

Description

A lovely blend of Pasta with Cheese which will fill your kitchen with a lovely aroma as it bakes. Any good quality hard strongish flavoured cheese will be an alternative to Double Gloucester if preferred. This quantity serves 4

Method

Stage 1

Cook the short cut Pasta in a Large saucepan of fast boiling water for about 10 minutes for dried Pasta, or 3 minutes for fresh Pasta, or until it is just tender. Drain well. While the Pasta is cooking, trim wash and chop the Leeks. Snip some Chives, and grate your cheese.

Stage 2

Melt the Butter in a frying pan, add the Leeks and fry them for 2 minutes to soften. Stir in the Flour and cook gently for a further minute whilst stirring. Remove from the heat and gradually stir in the Milk. Bring to the boil slowly and continue cooking, still stirring, until the sauce thickens. Remove from the heat and add all but 30ml (2 level tablespoons) of Grated Cheese, and the cooked Macaroni. Season to taste.

Stage 3

Spoon into a greased shallow, ovenproof dish. Mix together the Breadcrumbs, chopped Chives, and the remaining Cheese. Sprinkle across the top of the dish.

Stage 4

Bake in the oven at 190c (375f) Gas Mark 5 for 30 to 35 minutes until golden. Serve immediately.

Quick Guide

B C E F Q

Pepper Goulash

Mike Neville MBE

Ingredients

1 tbsp Olive Oil - 1 lb Potatoes

2 Medium Onions - 450g 1 lb Potatoes

1 tsp Caraway Seeds

2 tsp Ground Paprika - 2 tsp Cayenne Pepper

1 tbsp Plain Flour - 1 Red Pepper

250 ml / 8fl oz Vegetable Stock

400g can of Chopped Tomatoes

225g / 8 oz of Sweet Potatoes

225g / 8oz Vegetarian Steak

2 tbsp of Chopped Fresh Parsley

Description

Warming, and rib sticking. Mike says. "This sounds like my kind of food, I'll certainly be having a crack at it ! - being a dab hand in the kitchen !"

Method

Stage 1
Finely Slice Onions, chop up Pepper into medium sized pieces, cut Potatoes, and Sweet Potatoes into medium sized cubes, finely chop up Parsley

Stage 2
Heat the Olive Oil in a Large Pan. Add the Onions and cook slowly for 10 minutes until the Onions are soft and golden.

Stage 3
Add the chopped Pepper to the pan with the Caraway Seeds, Paprika, Cayenne, and Flour and cook for 1 minute whilst stirring.

Stage 4
Gradually stir in the Stock, and the Tomatoes, and bring to the boil. Stir in the Potatoes, and Sweet Potatoes, then cover and simmer for 10 - 15 mins.

Stage 5
Stir in the Vegetarian Steak, and the Parsley, Season to taste, and cook for a further 10 minutes.

Service

Spoon onto serving plates, and serve with a little Soured Cream or Yoghurt, and Crusty Bread.

Quick Guide

E   F   O   Q

Mushroom Gratin Bake

Thelma Barlow

Ingredients

6 oz of Mature Cheddar Cheese -- 6 oz of Broccoli Florets

2 Tablespoons of Sunflower Oil -- 1/2 Teaspoon of Sugar

8 oz of button Mushrooms -- Salt and Pepper to taste

1 Tablespoon Tomato Puree -- 1 Onion finely chopped

12 oz of Pasta Twist -- 1 Teaspoon of Oregano

2 Tablespoons of Chopped Fresh Parsley

2 drops of Tabasco -- 1 Clove of Garlic

14 oz can of Chopped Tomatoes

Description

This dish has a great number of ingredients which combine to make it really tasty. It is very easy to make, so why not give it a try !

Method

Stage 1

Cook the Pasta in boiling water according to the instructions on the packet. At the same time cook the Broccoli Florets in a pan of boiling water for about 5 minutes.

Stage 2

Finely Chop the Onion, and crush or finely chop the Garlic. Heat the Sunflower Oil in a frying pan, add the finely chopped Onion, and Garlic to the pan and cook slowly until they are softened.

Stage 3

Chop the Mushrooms into smallish pieces, add to the pan and cook for a further 3 - 4 minutes.

Stage 4

Pour the can of Chopped Tomatoes into the pan with the Sugar, Seasoning and Herbs, stir them then simmer slowly for 10 - 15 minutes.

Stage 5

Drain the cooked Pasta, and partly cooked Broccoli add these to the pan with the Tomato. Grate the Mature Cheddar Cheese into the pan.

Stage 6

Transfer to an oven proof dish. Place in a pre-heated oven at 190 c / 375 f, Gas Mark 5, for 25 minutes. Serve while hot

Quick Guide

B C E F

Courgette Spaghetti

Peter Sissons

Ingredients

Enough Spaghetti for two persons
(see the packet for quantities)

At least half a pound (224g) of fresh
Corgettes (the more the better)

Three or Four Tablespoons of good
quality Olive Oil.

Half a teaspoon of Garlic Puree, or
fresh Garlic if you have it to hand.

Salt and Black Pepper to taste

Fresh Parmesan Cheese.

Description

A simple recipe which can be made inside 20 minutes if you don't drain the Courgettes. Peter say's. "It is a great favourite of all my family. I could eat it every day"

Method

Stage 1

Wash the Courgettes then slice them thinly in the round. Dust with Salt and leave to drain for half an hour.

Stage 2

Bring large pan of water to the boil, then add sufficient Spaghetti for two persons (see packet for details), then continue to cook until the Spaghetti is cooked " al dente ", which means that there is just a bit of bite left in the middle.

Stage 3

Meanwhile, fry the Courgettes gently in a small quantity of Olive Oil (three or four tablespoons) with half a tea -spoon of Garlic Puree, or fresh Garlic stirred in. Add lots of freshly ground Black Pepper.

Stage 4

When the Courgettes are soft, and some may be turning brown, drain the cooked Spaghetti, then tip the cooked Courgettes into the pan of Spaghetti. Mix together well.

Stage 5

Add even more Black Pepper, and serve at once whilst still hot. As you serve the meal, grate fresh Parmesan Cheese on the top to finish.

Tip

This meal is very good in Winter or Summer with a glass of Valpolicella or Frascati. Also did you know that, "Olive Oil is good for your heart?"

Quick Guide

A C E F O Q

Leek and Aubergine Charlotte
with Sun Dried Tomatoes

Josceline Dimbleby

Ingredients

2 Tablespoons of Wine Vinegar

12 to 14 oz of Fresh Aubergines

1 1/2 lbs of Fresh Trimmed Leeks

1/2 teaspoon of Green Peppercorns

8 Sun-dried Tomatoes finely sliced

Sea Salt and Black Pepper to taste

approx. 300 ml (1/2 Pint) of Olive Oil

1 Large square white loaf,   sliced thinly

Description
A golden crisp bread crust encases a luscious filling of Leeks and Aubergines.

Method

Stage 1
Half fill a large saucepan with salted water, add the Wine Vinegar and bring to the boil. Whilst waiting for this to boil slice the Aubergine into rounds, and then cut it into cubes, adding them to the boiling water immediately they are cut. Stir the cubes then cover and boil briskly for two minutes. Once this is done, drain the pan completely and pat off excess water with kitchen paper.

Stage 2
Cut the Leeks across in 1 cm (1/2 inch) slices. Put four Tablespoons of the Olive Oil in a Large Heavy Saucepan over a Medium heat. Add the Leaks, Aubergine cubes, and Green Peppercorns. Stir the mixture then cover and cook for 10 to 15 minutes until the Leeks are soft. Then uncover the pan and continue to cook and stir for 1 to 2 mins. until all of the liquid is evaporated. Remove from the heat and stir in the Sun Dried Tomatoes, and season generously with the Sea Salt and Black Pepper.

Stage 3
Set the oven to Gas Mark 5, 190 c / 375 f. Oil a 1.5 Lt (2 1/2 pints) charlotte mould or cake tin. Pour the rest of the Olive Oil into a shallow dish. Cut the crusts off a slice of bread and dip the bread into the oil in the dish so that it is thoroughly smeared with oil on both sides. Lay the oiled bread in the bottom of the mould. Line the base with bread slices in this way, and continue up the sides overlapping the sides and bringing them up over the rim by about 2.5 cm (1 inch)

Stage 4
Spoon the Leek and Aubergine mixture into the lined mould packing it well down. Turn the overlapping edges of the bread over the top of the filling. Finally place further slices of bread over the top so that the filling is enclosed completely. (You may need extra oil to do this) put a metal plate or sandwich cake tin on top so that the bread edges won't curl up, but the air must be able to get in around the edges so that it does not steam.

Stage 5
Cook in the centre of the oven for one hour. Then turn out onto an oven-proof plate. Put the tin or plate back on the top and place the charlotte back in the oven for 10 -15 minutes, or until it is golden brown and crisp all over. It serves 4 to 5 persons.

Quick Guide

B E F

Root Vegetable Pie with Parsnip Pastry

Submitted by Josceline Dimbleby

Lots of ingredients hence no photograph but her photograph is shown with the previous recipe

Ingredients for the Pastry

375g (12 oz) of Parsnips, chopped -- 1 Teaspoon of Salt

2 Teaspoons of Baking Powder -- 300g (10 oz) of Plain Flour

175g (6 oz) of Butter cut into dice -- 1 Egg Yolk

Ingredients for the Filling

375g (12 oz) of Small Carrots -- 250g (8 oz) of diced Turnip

2 Teaspoons of Course Grain Mustard -- Salt and Black Pepper

3 Onions, sliced in rings -- 75 g (3 oz) of Butter

250g (8 oz) of Frozen Sweetcorn

1 Teaspoon of Ground Coriander

1 Rounded Teaspoon of Caraway Seeds

1 Rounded Tablespoon of Plain Flour

150 ml (1/4 Pint) of Soured Cream

300 ml (1/2 pint) of Cider

Description

Josceline say's. "I have a particular fondness for root vegetables during the chilly grey days of Winter. I find their sweet earthy flavours very soothing"

Method

Stage 1

To make the pastry. Boil the Parsnips in a pan of water until they are soft. Mash them thoroughly and leave to cool. Then sift the Flour and Baking Powder into a bowl and season well with Salt and Pepper. Rub the Butter into the Flour with your fingertips until it resembles Bread Crumbs. Stir in the cold mashed Parsnips until smooth. Wrap in cling film and refrigerate.

Stage 2

Blanch the Sweetcorn, drain and set to one side. Slice the Carrots and Turnips thinly. Then boil them in Salted Water until soft. Stir in the Coriander and Caraway Seeds, and remove from the heat. Then stir in the Mustard and Flour until smooth.

Stir in the Cider and return the pan to the heat. Bring to the boil, stirring, until the mixture thickens. Continue stirring for two minutes, then add the Sweetcorn. Remove from the heat, then stir in the Carrots, Turnips and Cream. Season to taste with Salt and Pepper, then turn the mixture into an oven-proof pie dish and leave to cool.

Stage 3

Using a floured rolling pin, roll out the Pastry on a lightly floured surface. Place the Pastry on top of the mixture in the pie dish, dampening the edges and pressing down well. Trim off any excess with a knife. Cut two small holes in the pastry to allow the steam to escape.

Stage 4

Refrigerate the pie until you are ready to cook it. Then brush with the Egg Yolk and cook in the centre of the oven, Gas Mark 6, 200 c / 400 f for about 25 minutes, or until the top is golden brown, and firm to touch
Serves 6 to 8 persons

Quick Guide

A   B   F   N   X

Herb Koulibiac

Rt Hon Sir Edward Heath KG MBE MP

<u>Ingredients</u>

6 oz of Cooked Rice (savory rice)

_____

2 Bunches of Spring Onions

_____

4 Hard Boiled Eggs -- 4 oz of Butter

_____

2 Tablespoons of chopped Parsley

_____

2 Tablespoons of chopped Chives

_____

2 Tablespoons of chopped Chervil

_____

4 oz of fresh Mushrooms -- 1 Egg yolk

_____

Sea Salt and Black Pepper to taste

_____

1 1/2 lbs of Short Crust Pastry

Description
A real Russian treat. It is easy to make, and it will freeze well.
Serve it hot with a creamy herb sauce and Red Wine if desired

Method

Stage 1
Boil 6 oz of Savory Rice in a pan of Water until it is fully cooked, soft and fluffy.
Drain and allow it to cool slightly. At the same time boil the 4 eggs for 5 minutes
to produce your hard boiled eggs. Allow them to cool slightly.

Stage 2
Half the 6 oz of Short Crust Pastry, and roll out each half into a rectangle 25 cm
x 20 cm (10" x 8"). Place one piece of rolled out pastry onto a lightly buttered
baking tray. (use approx. 1 oz of butter for this purpose)

Stage 3
Shell the boiled Eggs and cut them into thick slices. Trim the Spring Onions, and
slice them thinly. Wipe the Mushrooms with a clean damp cloth and slice them.

Stage 4
Melt 3 oz of the Butter in a sauce pan and cook the Sliced Mushrooms in the pan
briefly until they are soft. Then remove the Mushrooms from the Butter allowing
the excess butter to drain back into the pan. Mix the herbs with the cooked Rice.
Then put the Cooked Rice and Herb Mixture into the pan of melted Butter and mix
together well. The butter will now soak into the Rice and Herbs.

Stage 5
Lay the Boiled Rice mixture on top of the Short Crust Pastry on the baking tray.
Spread the Rice mixture out evenly on the pastry leaving a space of about 1"
around the edges. Lay the Sliced Boiled Eggs, sliced Mushrooms, and Sliced
Spring Onions on the top evenly. Season to taste with Sea Salt and Black Pepper..

Stage 6
Cover the top with remaining piece of Short Crust Pastry. Dampen the inner
edges of the Pastry with water, and seal the edges together firmly. Beat the
remaining Egg Yolk, then brush the outer pastry with the beaten Egg Yolk. Bake
in a moderately hot oven (200 c / 400 f) for about 25 minutes, or until golden
brown. Serve whilst still Hot.

Quick Guide

A   B   C   E   F

Mavis's Spinach Flans

Thelma Barlow

Ingredients

4 oz of Mature Cheddar Cheese
_____

2 oz of finely chopped Walnuts
_____

1 / 4 teaspoon of grated Nutmeg
_____

8 oz of Shortcrust Pastry
_____

Salt and Pepper to taste
_____

3 Tablespoons Cream
_____

1 Large beaten Egg
_____

8 oz Fresh Spinach

Description

A lovely combination of flavours. These small flans
are ideal for the buffet table,   packed lunch box or
a quick snack.   They can be served hot or cold.

Method

Stage 1
Pre-heat the oven to 200 C / 400 F, Gas Mark 6
Lightly grease either 4 Yorkshire Pudding Tins or
about 8 Patty Tins

Stage 2
Roll out the Shortcrust Pastry,   and put it into the
chosen sized Baking Tins. Use a knife to trim the
edges level with the rim of the tin.

Stage 3
Cook the Spinach in a pan of boiling water until it
is soft. Allow it to cool,   then chop it up very
finely. Chop the Walnuts into very small pieces,
grate the Cheese, and the Nutmeg. Beat the egg.

Stage 4
Mix together 3 oz of the Cheese, with the Cream,
the beaten Egg, Spinach, Nutmeg, Walnuts and
Salt and Pepper to taste.   Stir them together well.

Stage 5
Pour the mixture equally into the Pastry shells.
Place the remainder of the Grated Cheese onto
the top of the flans. Place in the Centre of the pre
-heated oven, and bake for 30 minutes,   or until
the the Pastry is Golden, and the filling is just firm.

Quick Guide

B   C   E   F

Spaghetti Dolce

Spike Milligan

Ingredients

5 oz Carton of Double Cream

---

2 Tablespoons of Brandy

Castor Sugar to taste

Enough un-cooked Spaghetti for
four people, (see packet for the
correct quantity.)

Description

This meal must be one of the quickest hot meals that we
have ever seen, and it is so very easy which means that
four persons can be eating in style in under 15 minutes !

This meal may be served with a crisp fresh side salad.

Method

Stage 1

Bring large pan of Water to the boil. Add the
Spaghetti, and cook it 'al dente', no added salt,
for about 8 minutes or until cooked (see packet)

Stage 2

Whilst the Spaghetti is cooking. Mix together the
Cream, Brandy, and Castor Sugar. This makes
up into a thick creamy sauce.

Stage 3

When it is cooked, share the Spaghetti onto four
plates. Pour Sauce over the top. Serve at once.

Quick Guide

C E N O Q X

* *

Beans on Toast
Submitted by Richard Branson

Fun for the kids

Ingredients

1 x 15 oz tin of Baked Beans

Small quantity of Butter or Margarine

---

2 x Large Slices of White or Brown Bread

Method

Heat Baked Beans in a medium sized pan, meanwhile toast
two slices of bread. Spread the Butter onto the toast when
it is toasted. Add previously heated beans. Serve whilst hot

C   E   G   Q

Potato Gratin (Gratin Savoyard)

Ronnie Corbett OBE

Ingredients

1 Pint (600 ml) of Double Cream

Freshly Ground White Pepper

Freshly Ground Sea Salt

Freshly Grated Nutmeg

1 / 2 a Clove of Garlic

4 Tablespoons of Milk

1 1/2 lbs of Potatoes
(Medium Sized)

Description

Ronnie Say's. "This is a Classic Potato Gratin which can easily be prepared in advance. With it's delicious blend of garlic and nutmeg and it's moist creamy texture, this dish re-heats very well in a slow oven." So why don't you try it ?

Method

Stage 1

Slice the Potatoes very thinly to a thickness of only 1/10th of an inch (2mm) using a mandoline or very sharp knife. Then spread the Potato slices on a flat surface and sprinkle them with the Sea Salt. Mix them together well so that all of their surfaces are covered with Salt. Then leave them in a pile for about 10 minutes

Stage 2

Dip the 1/2 Clove of Garlic in the Sea Salt to draw out the juices. Prepare an oven proof Gratin Dish by rubbing the inside of the dish with the Garlic. Pre-heat the oven to 250 f / 120 c

Stage 3

Heat the Cream and the Milk together in a saucepan which is large enough to hold all of the slices of Potato. Add the White Pepper and the Nutmeg to taste. Bring the Cream and Milk to the boil and boil for several minutes over a high heat. (Watching it continuously in case it boils over.)

Stage 4

Shake the Salt, and any water which the Salt will have drawn out of the Potato Slices off the Potato Slices. Add the Potatoes to the Cream / Milk mixture in the pan. Bring back to the boil and then immediately remove from the heat. Using a draining spoon, with care lift the Potato Slices from the pan into the Gratin Dish. Try to arrange them evenly in layers cover these with the Cream mixture.

Stage 5

Bake for about 45 minutes, until the Potatoes are tender and the Cream has formed a Golden Brown Crust. Serve whilst still hot.

Quick Guide

B E F N

Filo pastry tarts filled with wild mushrooms served with a lemon and chive hollandaise

Submitted by HRH The Duchess of York

Ingredients

Filo Pastry

---

6 oz of Butter

---

1 Tablespoon of Wine Vinegar

---

3 Large Egg Yolks

A pinch of Salt

---

2 - 3 Tablespoons of Lemon Juice

Some Freshly Chopped Chives

Description

A real Royal recipe packed full to the brim with good taste.   It's quite complicated, but well worth the effort. A good recipe for people who expect the very best of food, and like to have their taste buds tickled.

Method

Stage 1

Baking the Filo Pastry Tart Shells :- Cut the Filo Pastry into squares which are slightly larger than the chosen individual mini flan dishes. Line each flan dish with four or five sheets of Filo Pastry,   brushing each sheet of pastry with melted Butter between the sheets. Overlap

Stage 1 (continued)

each sheet, and drape over the sides of the tin to achieve a flower effect. Bake in a moderate oven until golden brown and crisp.

Stage 2

The Wild Mushroom filling is made as follows:- Saut'e a selection of Wild Mushrooms that have been chopped up finely in a pan with the melted Butter until they are soft and well cooked through. Season with Salt and Pepper to taste.

Stage 3

Making the Lemon and Chive Hollandaise Sauce. In one sauce pan heat and melt the 6 oz of Butter. Place the Wine Vinegar and Lemon Juice in a second saucepan, bring them slowly to the boil. Blend the Egg Yolks in a food processor, and with the rotor still running, very gradually add the hot Vinegar and Lemon Juice mixture. Then bring the pan of melted Butter to the boil, and add it in a thin trickle into the mixture which is already in the food processor until it is all added and the sauce is thickened. Season to taste with Salt and Pepper. Don't be afraid to add more Lemon if it is thought necessary. Then add the Chopped Chives.

To Serve

Fill the Filo Tarts with the Mushroom mixture and serve immediately. Put a serving of Lemon Chive Hollandaise to one side of each tart.

Safety Warning

Wild Mushrooms are wonderful provided that you know just what you are doing. Don't just wander off into the woods to pick and use anything that you find, or you may be very seriously ill. If in doubt, purchase your Wild Mushrooms from a reliable stockist.

Quick Guide

A   B   D   N   T

Killer Chilli

Submitted by Lenny Henry

Ingredients

2 Big Onions -- 2 Green Peppers

---

1 15 oz tin of Italian Tomatoes -- Tomato Puree

---

1 15 oz tin of Kidney Beans -- A pinch of Cloves

A pinch of Oregano -- A pinch of Mixed Spices

A dash of Tabasco -- A glass of Red Wine

---

2 Vegetable Stock Cubes -- 1/4 lb of Mushrooms

---

1 lb of Vegetarian Mince -- A Lucky Rabbits Foot ?

Chilli Powder mild or not depending if your tongue is made of leather !

Description

As you would expect this recipe is a blend of humour and good taste.
Lenny say's. "Hang the Lucky Rabbits Foot around your neck because
you'll need all the luck you can get because I don't know what I'm doing.

Method

Chop up the Onions and Green Peppers. Put in a frying pan with some
Butter. Fry them slowly until the Onions are translucent (that means see
through, thicky). Add the Vegetarian Mince and fry until it is brown.
Add the Tomatoes and stir for a couple of minutes until it is hot and
bubbling noisily. Add about 1 Tbsp of Tomato Puree and stir until the
sauce thickens. Add all the Spices and Herbs, chop the Mushrooms
add them and stir for 2 minutes. Add the Kidney Beans and give a good
stir. Add a dash of Tabasco and crumble in the stock cubes. Put the wine
in and stir again. Put on a very low heat and allow to simmer for about an
hour stirring occasionally. After this time it should be a lovely dark brown
colour and quite thick. Serve with Rice or Pitta Bread.

Northumberland Mental Health HNS Trust

Northumberland Mental Health Trust is the main provider of NHS services for people with mental health problems in Northumberland. We aim to provide the support and care that people with mental health problems need and to help them resume their everyday lives within their own communities.

Northumberland Mental Health NHS Trust

Chairman's Pudding

Mohamed Al Fayed, Chairman of Harrods

Ingredients

1 Pint Milk (full fat or semi-skimmed)

---

1 Pint Whipping Cream

---

26 g Caster Sugar

---

4 x Egg Yolks (size 2)

---

2 x Whole Eggs (size 2)

---

100 g Sultanas

---

70 g of Butter

Small loaf of white bread
medium sliced (app. 16 slices)

Description

A 'First Class' Bread Pudding. Just the thing to warm you through
on a Cold Winters Day. But why wait for winter ? Serves 4 - 6

Method

Stage 1

Sprinkle half of the Sultanas into the bottom
of a medium sized oven proof dish.

Stage 2

Remove the crusts from bread slices and cut
into diagonal quarters. Arrange the diagonal
quarters in the dish, overlapping each layer
and placing small cubes of butter between
each layer as you go. Keep going in this
fashion until the bowl is filled.

Stage 3

Pour the milk and cream into a pan and bring
to the boil. Whisk Egg Yolks, Eggs and
Caster Sugar until well mixed. Then add hot
milk and cream mixture and blend together

Stage 4

Pour hot mixture over bread in oven proof
dish. Sprinkle top with remaining Sultanas.
Place ovenproof dish in a baking tray which is
half filled with warm water. Cook in oven at
150C/300F/ Gas Mark 2 for approx 50 min.
or until the top is golden brown.

Serving Suggestions.   This pudding is best served hot with one of
Mr. Fayed's favourite sauces. The sauces may be served hot or cold.

Raspberry Sauce

Puree and sieve 200 g (7oz) of fresh Raspberries. Bring to the boil 75g
(3oz) sugar and 75 ml (2 1/2 fl oz) Red Burgundy with 1 slice of lemon
rind. Add the Raspberry Puree, and reduce for about 3 - 4 minutes.

Apricot Sauce

Blanch, skin and stone 250 g (9 oz) of ripe Apricots. Puree in a blender
with 7 tablespoons of sugar syrup (boil equal amounts of water and
sugar for 3 - 4 minutes). Stir in 2 teaspoons of fresh lime juice.

Quick Guide

B E F N X

The Lord of Barton's Pudding

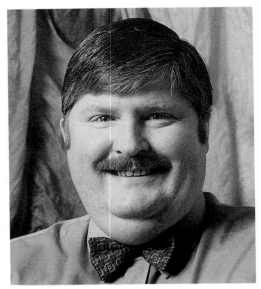

Arnold Baker Esq, Lord of Barton

Ingredients

8 oz unsalted Butter

---

8 oz Soft Flour

---

4 Eggs

The Seeds from 1 Vanilla Pod

---

2 Teaspoons of Baking Powder

1/2 Teaspoon of Ground Cinnamon

'Grand Marnier' (Alcoholic Liquor)

---

4 oz of Fresh Blueberries

Description

A delightfully light flavour-some sponge pudding
which is greatly enhanced if it is served with a
light orange flavoured custard sauce

Method

Stage 1

Marinate 4 oz of Saltanas and 4 oz of Blueberries
in a small quantity of Gran Marnier for 24 hours

Stage 2

Cream together the 8 oz of unsalted butter with 8 oz
of Vanilla Sugar. Add 12 oz of soft flour 4 eggs, 2 x
Teaspoons of Ground Cinnamon, and the seeds from
1 x Vanilla Pod. Whisk together well

Drain marinated Saltanas and Blueberries of excess
fluid. Fold marinated fruit into the above mixture

Stage 3

Steam for 40 minutes in buttered and sugared
'Ramekins'

Serving Suggestions

This pudding is best served Piping Hot surrounded
with a thin 'Orange flavoured' Anglaise (Custard)

Garnish (Optional)

Grate the zest of an orange onto the top of the
sponge before serving for optinum presentation

Quick Guide

A F N S X

Orange and Lemon Flan

Margaret, The Lady Thatcher, O.M., P.C., F.R.S.

Ingredients

1 x 9 inch pre-baked Pastry Tart Shell

For the filling

2 Large Eggs & 3 oz (3/8 cup) Castor Sugar

4 fl oz (1/2 cup) of Single Cream

The grated zest, and juice of 1 small Orange.

A few drops of Almond Essence

For the Topping

2 large thin skinned Lemons & 3 oz(3/8 cup)Sugar

2 small thin skinned Oranges & 5 fl oz(5/8 cup) Water

4 tablespoons of sieved Marmalade or Orange Jelly

Description

A tangy Lemon and Orange flan. Just the thing to boost your vitamin C intake.
Serve it warm or cold with an accompanying jug of cream.(Serves 6 - 8)

Method

Stage 1

Heat the oven to 375 f / 190 c (gas mark 5)

Stage 2

Whisk the eggs and 3 oz of Castor Sugar together until thick and creamy. Add Single Cream, the grated zest, and juice of 1 small Orange, and a few drops of Almond Essence. Beat vigorously until well mixed

Stage 3

Spread the mixture in the pre-baked pastry tart shell and bake in the oven for 30-40 minutes until it is well risen, golden, and firm to the touch in the centre.

Stage 4

Prepare the topping by slicing the Oranges and Lemons very thinly, removing the pips. If the pith of the fruit is thick, peel it off with a sharp knife as you would an apple or they may be rather bitter.

Stage 5

Dissolve the 3 oz of Sugar in the Water in a shallow pan and bring to the boil. Lay the Orange and Lemon slices in the syrup and simmer for 3 minutes, then remove them and drain well. Boil the remaining syrup until it is reduced by half. Stir in the Marmalade or Orange Jelly and heat until it is completely melted to give a good, rich glaze

Stage 6

Arrange the Orange and Lemon slices on top of the tart and brush generously with the glaze. Place the tart under a hot grill for a few minutes until the glaze is bubbling & caramelised

B E G N O

Apple and Cinnamon Slice

The Rt Hon The Lord Jeffrey Archer

Ingredients

Sponge and Topping

6 oz / 175g Self-raising Flour

1 tsp / 5 ml Baking Powder

4 oz / 125g Caster Sugar

4 oz / 125g   Butter or Margarine

6 fl oz / 175 ml of Milk

1 Egg, beaten ------ Pinch of Salt

3 - 4 Medium Sized Eating Apples

Half tsp / 2.5 Ground Cinnamon

1 tbsp / 15 ml Clear Honey

Description

Good Lord. This Apple and Cinnamon Slice
can be made, and eaten, in about one hour!

Method

Stage 1
Pre-heat the Oven to Mark 6 / 400 F / 200 C

Stage 2
Sieve the Self-raising Flour, Baking Powder and
Salt together. Stir in the Caster Sugar and rub in
the Butter or Margarine.

Stage 3
Beat the Egg, and combine with the Milk, and mix
with the flour mixture until it forms a smooth batter.
Pour the batter into an 8" / 20cm Square Cake Tin

Stage 4
Core, peel and thickly slice the Eating Apples and
then press the pieces lightly into the batter mixture
in the tin.

Stage 5
Sprinkle the Ground Cinnamon over the apple slices
and bake in the pre-heated oven for 40 - 45 minutes
or until sponge is springy and firm to the touch.

Stage 6
Using a pastry brush, brush the top of the cake evenly
with Clear Honey to glaze. Remove from the tin while
it is still warm. Cut into portions with a sharp knife

Tip
This apple slice can be served hot or cold It serves 8.
Preparation time 10 minutes. Cook: 40 - 45 minutes

B C E F N Q

Bread and Butter Pudding

Anthea Turner

Ingredients

12 Large Slices of White Bread

8 Egg Yolks

3/4 of a Pint of Double Cream (450 ml)

1/4 of a Pint of Milk (150 ml)

6 oz of Caster Sugar (150 g)

1 Vanilla Pod

2 oz of mixed Sultanas and Raisins (50 g)

A small quantity of Icing Sugar. (to dust top)

Description

Even if you haven't won the lottery, you can still be a winner with this classic pudding. It's just the thing to enjoy all year round, but it is a particular family favourite over the winter months.

Method

Stage 1

Remove the crusts from the bread and discard them. Spread the Butter onto the bread. Cut the remaining bread into large squares. Layer the bottom of an oven-proof dish with these squares of bread.

Stage 2

Sprinkle the top of the bread with some of the mixed Saltanas and Raisins. Continue in this fashion laying the bread and fruit into layers until all of the bread and fruit is in the oven-proof dish

Stage 3

Put the Milk and the Cream into a large saucepan add the Vanilla pod, then bring the mixture to the boil, stirring occasionally.

Stage 4

Put the Egg Yolks into a bowl, add the Caster Sugar, whisk together. Add this mixture to the Milk mixture in the pan. Stir, remove the Vanilla Pod, and then pour the combined mixture into the Oven-proof dish containing the Bread and Fruit.

Stage 5

Sit the dish in a "bain marie". Cover and place in a Warm Oven, Gas Mark 2, 120c / 320f for 30 to 40 minutes until just set. Remove from the Oven and dust with Icing Sugar, or a little Caster Sugar and place under a hot grill to glaze.

"bain marie"

Note: a bain marie, means a warm water bath. Simply place the bread and butter pudding dish in a slightly larger oven-proof dish containing water which rises half to three quarters of the way up the bread and butter dish. This allows the pudding to cook slowly and evenly.

Quick Guide

Sweet Potato ~ Apple Pie

Alan Robson MBE

Ingredients

3/4 lb of Short Crust Pastry Mix

_____

1 Large Sweet Potato and 1 Large Sweet Apple

_____

1/8 Cup of Sweet Orange, Pineapple, or Apple Juice

_____

1/4 Cup of Light Brown Sugar (packed)

_____

1/4 Teaspoon of Cinnamon

_____

1/8 Teaspoon Ginger and Nutmeg combined

_____

1/4 Cup of finely ground Blanched Almonds
or 1/4 cup of Dried Coconut.

Description

A Sweet Heavy Desert which when it is made without Sugar
and the Pie Crust, can be a tasty side dish to a main meal.

Method

Stage 1

Pre-heat the Oven to 200 degrees Celsius

Stage 2

Bake the Sweet Potato to soften, then Peel

Stage 3

Mash the Sweet Potato in a large mixing bowl.
Peel the Sweet apple and grate it into the bowl.

Stage 4

Add chosen juice, and all other dry ingredients.
Mash together to mix well, and spoon into an
8" Oven proof Dish

Stage 5

Make up Short Crust Pastry, then roll it out into a
crust. Put crust onto the top of the Oven proof dish.
Brush the top of the pie with Milk or Egg White.

Stage 6

Bake in the oven for 30 - 40 minutes, or until the
crust is nicely browned and the prongs of a fork
poked into the centre come out clean. Allow to
stand for 10 minutes then serve.

Quick Guide

B C E F Q

The Very Best Chocolate Cake

Debbie Thrower

Cake Ingredients

2 oz (50g) Cocoa

_____

6 Tablespoons of Boiling Water

_____

3 Eggs (size 2)

_____

4 Fl oz of Milk

_____

6 oz (175g) of Self Raising Flour

_____

1 Rounded Teaspoon of Baking Powder

_____

4 oz (100g) Soft Baking Margarine

_____

10 oz Castor Sugar

Description
Chocolate cake is a firm favourite for many people. Debbie
describes this cake as the 'Very Best'. So start Baking!

Icing and Filling Ingredients
4 1/2 oz (125g) Good Chocolate

_____

3 Tablespoons of Apricot Jam

_____

5 fl oz of Double Cream

_____

Method
Cake Baking. Stage 1
Grease two 8" round sandwich cake tins.
Line the base's with Grease Proof Paper
Stage 2
Mix the Cocoa with Boiling Water in a Food Processor until
it is well mixed. Then add the remaining cake ingredients to the
Food Processor and whiz for 1 - 2 minutes, scraping down
the mixture if necessary. The mixture will be a thickish batter.
Stage 3
Divide the cake mixture equally between the prepared cake tins.
Bake at 350 F / 180 C / Gas mark 4, until well risen and
shrinking away from the sides of the tin, about 20 minutes.

Cake Finishing Method
Stage 1
Measure the Chocolate and Cream together in a bowl and stand
the bowl in a pan of simmering water for approx. 10 - 15 mins.
Stirring from time to time until Chocolate has melted. Then
allow this mixture to become cold and almost set.
Stage 2
Spread the tops of each cake with Apricot Jam. Fill the cakes with
half the icing, and spread the remainder on the top with pallet knife.

B E F N O

Apple Fruit Cake

Edwina Currie MP

Ingredients

100 g (4oz) of Plain Flour -- 2 medium sized Eggs

---

100 g (4oz) of Wholemeal Flour

The grated rind of a Lemon

---

150 g (6oz) of soft Brown Sugar

---

1 tsp of Mixed Spice -- 100 g (4oz) of Margarine

---

125 g (5oz) of Currants -- 125 g (5oz) of Raisins

1/2 tsp of Coriander -- 50 g (2oz) Mixed Peel

---

225 g (8oz) of Cooking Apples

Description

An unusual version of a standard fruit cake. The apples add lightness and moisture. This recipe produces about 20 slices of cake. Each slice has about 160 kcals, and 5 g of Fat, Sodium 60mg, and 1 g of Fibre.Preperation and Cooking Time 1 hour 35 minutes

Method

Stage 1

Pre-heat oven to 180 C (350 F). Grease and line a 20 cm(8") Round "Deep" Cake Tin with buttered grease proof paper

Stage 2

Sift plain Flour, Soda and Spices into a bowl and mix in the Wholemeal Flour

Stage 3

Cream the Margarine and Sugar together in a separate mixing bowl, beat in the eggs one at a time following each with a tablespoon of the Flour mixture. Fold in the remaining flour mixture

Stage 4

Grate the rind of Lemon, and the Cooking Apples add them to the mixture with the Dried Fruit. Mix together well.

Stage 5

Spoon the mixture into the prepared cake tin. Level the top, then bake just below the centre of the oven for about 1 1/4 hours. Remove from the oven then let the cake settle in the tin for about 10 minutes before turning out onto a wire cooling rack.

Quick Guide

B C E F N

Carrot Fruit Cake

Claire Rayner

<u>Ingredients</u>

225 g (8 oz) of Self-Raising Flour

---

175 g (6 oz) of Butter or Margarine

---

225 g (8 oz) of Caster Sugar

---

2 Teaspoons of Cinnamon

---

2 Large Eggs -- a Pinch of Salt

---

225 g (8 oz) of Grated Carrots

---

225 g (8 oz) of Chopped Walnuts

---

225 g (8 oz) of Chopped Dates

Description

Claire say's. "This cake is a bit common or garden, but it's a sizeable family cake made from Carrots, Nuts, and Fruit. It's of the cut and come again variety, and it keeps well if the family will let you !"

Method

Stage 1

Chop Walnuts, and Dates into small pieces. Toss the Dates in a small quantity of Icing Sugar if you have it to stop them clumping together. (Caster Sugar will do instead of Icing Sugar if you have none) Wash, Peel, and Grate the Carrots.

Stage 2

Mix Flour, Cinnamon, and a Pinch of Salt together in a mixing bowl. Then cream together the Butter and Caster Sugar in a separate bowl until it is thick and fluffy. Beat the Eggs and add them gradually to the Butter and Sugar mix. Stir together well.

Stage 3

Slowly stir the Flour, Cinnamon, and Salt mixture into the creamed Butter, Caster Sugar, and Egg mix, beating well to ensure that the mixture is smooth.

Stage 4

Finally add the Grated Carrots, Chopped Dates, & Walnuts Mix evenly throughout the mixture.

Stage 5

Turn mixture into a lined or well greased cake tin. Level out. Then bake in the middle of a Moderate Oven (180 c / 350f) Gas Mark 4, until the top is well browned and it springs back if you press it. About 45 minutes to 1 hour depending on how your oven behaves.

Quick Guide

B C E F N

Bara Brith

Sir Anthony Hopkins

Ingredients

1 lb of Self-Raising Flour

---

6 oz of Brown Sugar

1/2 Pint of Warm Strained Tea

---

1 Large Beaten Egg

---

1 Teaspoon of Mixed Spice

---

2 Tablespoons of Course
Cut Orange Marmalade

---

1 lb of Mixed Dried Fruit
Currants, Sultanas, Raisins

Description

Bara Brith is a recipe from Wales. It produces a rich fruit loaf which will keep well. Serve it sliced with Butter or Margarine.

Method

Stage 1

Make a nice pot of tea and pour yourself a cup let the remainder stew to a good strength. Pour half a Pint of this Tea whilst it is still warm into a mixing bowl, and add to it the Mixed Fruit, and Brown Sugar. Stir together and allow this mixture to stand covered overnight to marinate.

Stage 2

Sieve the Self-Raising Flour, and Mixed Spice into a mixing bowl. Warm the Marmalade until it is liquid and runny. Then add the Marmalade to the Flour and Spice. Mix it all together well.

Stage 3

Beat the Egg, then add it to the mixture. Stir it all together again.   Then add the Marinated Mixed Fruit,   Sugar and Tea. Mix all of this together well.

Stage 4

Pour Mixture into a lined or greased loaf tin. Level out the mixture.

Stage 5

Bake in an oven for about 1 1/2 hours at Gas Mark 4 (180 c / 350 F) or until it is well risen, and the top is browned and firm to the touch. Remove from the oven,   leave for ten minutes then turn it out onto a wire cooling rack to cool.

Quick Guide

A B C E F N

Apple~Nut Crumble

Submitted by The Lady Patience Baden-Powell CBE

Ingredients

2 lbs of Fresh Cooking Apples

White Sugar to sweeten to taste

---

3 ozs of Plain Flour -- 3 ozs of Butter

---

3 ozs of Roasted Chopped Hazel Nuts

---

3 ozs of Brown Sugar

Description

A very traditional pudding, in which you have to use your own discretion as to how much sugar to use according to your taste, and the degree of tartness of the apples. Serve with a jug of cream or some custard. It's very easy to make.

Method

Stage 1

Peel and core the Apples and cut them into thin slices. Then in a pan with a very small amount of water bring to the boil and simmer very slowly until they are slightly softened. Then remove from the heat and sweeten with the Sugar until they are sweetened but still sharp and slightly tart or under sweet. Arrange the apples in a baking dish.

Stage 2

Rub the Flour and Butter together with your fingers in a mixing bowl. Add Nuts and Brown Sugar. Mix together well. This is your Crumble Mix. Put this mix evenly on the top of the Apples in the baking dish. Bake in a Moderate Oven, for 10 - 15 minutes or until the top is Crunchy and Browned. Serve whilst hot.

Quick Guide

B   C   E   F   N   Q

Adrian Mole's Scones

Submitted by Sue Townsend, aged 44 and 3/4

Ingredients

4 oz of Self Raising Flour or metric equivalent

_____

2 oz of Butter or metric equivalent

_____

2 oz of Sugar or metric equivalent

_____

1 egg (eggs are still eggs)

Description

The warm smell of baking does not greet me as I enter the kitchen. So I create my own by baking scones. Here is Adrians recipe for plain scones.

Method

Stage 1

Preheat the oven to Gas Mark 5. Put all of the above ingredients into a mixing bowl, and mix them together well to form a thick dough.

Stage 2

Roll out the dough to a thickness of approximately 1/2 to 3/4 of an inch. Cut to shape with a scone cutter or sharp knife. Place onto a lightly greased baking tray, and bake in the oven until they have risen well, and are a light golden colour. Usually about 12 minutes. Keep opening the oven door to check the progress. Remove from the oven then allow to cool on wire rack

Some other options

To make Cheese Scones add grated Cheese to the dough. To make Fruit Scones add some Raisins or Sultanas to the dough.

Quick Guide

B C E F N O Q

About the Author

Arnold Baker

Arnold Baker was born in Iserlohn, Germany in 1950. He came to settle in Newcastle in 1952 with his family, when his father completed his military service. Having been educated in Newcastle where he gained qualifications in building construction at Charles Trevellian Technical College (now called Newcastle College), and business studies at Newcastle Poly -technic (now called Northumbria University at Newcastle) He became governor of four inner City schools in Newcastle. He now lives at Wark, near Hexham, Northumberland.

In 1972 Arnold joined Northumberland Constabulary (now Northumbria Police) and served as a Police Officer until 1989, when his career was curtailed when he was retired after having sustained a series of injuries in the execution of his police duties. Whilst serving the community as a Police Officer, he was well known in the media as 'Northumbria Police's Famous Shrinking Policeman', because of his charitable efforts in numerous areas.

In 1990 he was appointed Regional Director of A.C.T. In retirement he continued to serve the community in very many areas in charitable efforts to raise much needed funding for such worthy causes as hospitals, medical research, and private individuals facing great difficulty.

1996 marks the 25th. Anniversary of the start of Arnold Bakers charitable contribution to the community. It is fitting that this book links with that notable event. In producing this book he hopes that he can greatly help the Opus Project to move positively towards the Millennium.

Arnold Baker is the 21st. Lord of Barton. (Cambridge) As successor to this hereditary title he was greatly honoured when he received a grant of Arms in his own right from the Crown in 1993. He was honoured to receive the Freedom of the City of London in 1993.

Christine Baker